He wished to become the human he longed to be

BY ADITHYA KRISHNAKUMAR

About the author

A quiet observer of moments and emotions, Adithya KrishnaKumar writes with a heart that listens more than it speaks. a lifelong lover of stories, he finds poetry in fleeting glances, whispered conversations, and the spaces between silence.

His words often walk barefoot through love, longing, growth, and the gentle ache of memory. This debut collection is a reflection of his own journey — the people he met, the feelings he couldn't say out loud, and the truth he found in verse.

When he's not writing, you might find him watching sunsets, or tucking away new poems in the corners of his journal — always chasing meaning, one line at a time.

To my folks and to who had to see and endure
me since day 1

To the authors of my folks

To my teachers, ashok mama,mitu and chechi
for leaving a bundle of hope without sheading a
sweat

To the one who asked me to start poetry and to
never give up on it on a dusty cricket field back
in 2022.

To the boys for never letting me down

And finally to achyuth the realest piece of
human I could ever wish more than a brother
for sure

He wished to become the human he longed to be

1. Her blood and her bones

My love what have I done?

The world you opened in front of me has been shattered once again

Just like in the nightmares we saw

And the drinks and smoke we saved are once again in the drain

Why are we here again?

Are we really here?

Or is it our mind playing battles just like the old days?

Your sword is set to strike my cardboard

But ask yourself this question

Did we travel this much just to throw it all in the
fire

Are you really telling me we walked miles just to
stop before the finish line

Your blood is all over my face just like you
wanted it to be.

And your bones are all over my place just like
hoped

And yet I am standing here hoping you would
back

It was only yesterday when I feasted on your
eyes

It was only yesterday when you asked me to
stay

It was only yesterday when we put out the
flame

It was only yesterday when your lips tasted like
cigarette stains

And here you are believing everything you see

Planning my funeral like never before

And to question your thoughts I think I am worthy

But is he?

Give me a another night of your sight

Let it be my mind says

But my mind doesn't know my heart

And why did we throw it all away?

Did the devil tempt you?

With his blood and your bones?

Did you make a deal with him?

To fight the devil I have no power

But remember the devil

As he can change everything just like you change your coat.

I can't fight the devil as I don't have his ruthlessness

But remember who the bigger man is

And who the devil is.

2. THE GLOURIOUS MORNING

The daylight is right above her eyes

While I stand here taking a look at the ice

Will I find the might to break the ice?

Or will she fall into the bottomless pit he
planned for her

She planned glorious mornings for my hunt

But he wasn't my prey

Until he broke pact

Words abused and our hands refused to speak

While the world claimed it's all over

The devil arises from his grave

As he know that there is darkness inside every
man who tries to speak the truth

Yet his lies were like the glorious morning

Impeccable yet hard to digest

If I was the prey all along then why did she load
my gun?

Why did he scar the place he built?

Words exchanged and the blood he owed
became the blood he saved

The blood is all over her face but since the
nightfall her face and words aren't like a
glorious morning

And the night is all around us

The ice won't break it is hard just like his hands

I might lack the skills he might posses

But I don't lack the heart he doesn't have

To live like a human and not like a shark

I must end this blood lust once and for all

The glorious morning will shine just like how she
planned

But she won't be there

The world knows he will be in a deranged world
of his own devouring meds, fighting loosing
battles

To see the glorious morning see must have a clear battle with herself

While I the poet who spilled his blood for rage might be the one they seek in the future for success

The day shall come when we will rise while the devil shall burn in his grave

The day shall come when she wins the battle and sees the glorious morning

While I shall be regaining my blood from the ashes...

3. LOST WORDS

The drinks we had are down the sink

Your words struck me like a knife

Will I find a shelter while you wage your
hurricane?

The nights are over your head like my tears

Or is this just a another way of wickedness

Will you visit your thoughts again?

Or will you kick me out of my chair

Once again I shall hear your lost mind

I don't know if you are the devil incarnate

I don't know if you are the devil

I don't know if you are the reaper

I don't know if you are my brother

But I do know that there's a side where mercy
and kindness is a sin

Let it be

But what about the blood you owed me for the
darkness I done for you

I won't let that go in the drain

The devil can't stop me

The devil is in you I can sense it

But never will he conquer the world with your
lost words

4. THE WAR WE WAGE

It's that time of the year again

Broken homes and broken hearts are yet to be mended

As we come together once again

Another year has passed down the drain

Before we mend our self lets recall our fallen poets

The poets who stood for our dreams

Even when the world turned their back on us

Its time to forget the world but not their actions

This day marks the end of the long battle

And the blood we lost are nothing but pain and misery

Never forget the one who waged the war

Who would that be the world asks?

The one who waged this lonely war is none other than our precious devil himself

Isn't he satisfied with his envy?

Hasn't he poisoned enough souls?

Once again the devil walks among us

The people will start raising their voice saying

Why does he have to interfere in this holy day?

But now the people aren't afraid of this so
called devil

When the devil sights graze over their eyes they
won't fight him

They will simply raise their cup for their first and
last time

Because they have tasted the warmth of
knowing that

The poet inside of them will wage their war

The world of a poet is enormous yet small

The world of a poet is beautiful yet gloomy

The world of a poet is rich yet poor

The world of a poet is nothing but his sword and
his sword is nothing but his mind

The word of a poet is stronger than a dragons breath

Fiercer than any venom

Stronger than the devils fire

As the battle comes to an end the poet is almost dead

But his death means a lot

Due to his courage

The people shall rebel

The people shall raise their voice

And they will paint their flag before their term

Let the poet inside us

Massacre the devil inside of us

5. LITTLE ONE AND HIS WORLD

He wakes up with pain

But little did he know

The pain he felt is going to heal

Yet scar

He pulls his head and makes his hair

The little one won't let them see

As he knows it would be bleeding among sharks

He walks away to an world of misery

The world is yet to be complete

He asks himself where the missing piece would be

But little did he know it was with him the whole time

He forgot to cast them

He makes his mind and walks towards wickedness

He spoke to deranged people

And his words were like a shelter to them

The devil saw him and commanded to kneel

But he didn't he never bowed before any god

He knew he was the one who is supposed to wage the war against him

His scars reminds him of a time where he
thought he could conquer the world

He walks towards the devil with a smile

He sucks all the pain he ever felt

He moves on and on

He bears it day by day

Hour by hour

The scar will remain

Until the devil is dead

6. DERANGED ROADS AND ME

These deranged roads I can't see a thing except
the devil
Who is plotting among the clouds
Will the night stay forever?
Or is it just a glimpse of time
Which is there for me?

I can't say anything, I don't know anything
I don't know if I am going to survive the night
I don't know if I have what it takes to fight the
devil
The devil plans a funeral for me

A funeral where I am not dead
A funeral where there is no wine
A funeral where there is no coffin
A funeral where I am alive
A funeral where she is there to touch my lips
which I can't feel
A funeral full of lies
A funeral where I am buried alive

And when I am six feet under
I understand that I am the devil who plotted
everything against me

There is no devil, there is no human
There is only righteous and sins
And I became the master of sins
And I find my comfort here

7. THE ROAD

He packed his bag and stood empty in the face
of the road

To find time he yearned

To walks his legs waited

But he was too heavy for his legs to carry him

To move forward and answer his heart

He stood without turning back

His road didn't lead him to any heaven

Nor hell was found

But he found people and he found comfort in
strangers arm

Every kiss felt like an arrow

Every thrust was leading him nowhere

And he packed his bags once again

But this time he had a destination on his mind

It was his pal's grave

To see him once again before he took his final trip

And finally lay near his eyes

His feet were wet but his arms were dry as a bone

And he was with him in a quiet sunny day where even the chilliest beer could boil

Why this road?

His real bag never left his grave it was he who travelled through me

8. A THROWBACK TO THE PAST

He found his broken palace in her arms

When he laid there by her side

She smiled like never before

She wasn't about to taste him

She wasn't about to feel him

She knew words

Those words became people

People became humans

Humans became ashes

And finally ashes

Became words once again

As she kept

Fiddling through

His hair

She found a world where she was dead

She knew they both want one thing and one thing only

To grow

To live

To cry

To face the wrath

Of their own

And to lay indefinitely

Coffins weren't made for them

Funerals wasn't planned

They didn't wish to get buried

They wished to see

They wished to feel

And their wishes became just like ocean salts

Washed ashore

Used by someone else

9. Where will he stand?

In the darkness he stood

As he was always limited there

By who?

The world and their words?

It wasn't the world or their words

But ideas and norms made him

Stay in the corner

Like a kid who is facing time out

Like a soldier who is processing

The concept of death

Like a convicted waiting for the rope

 He stood

He knew to stand is to speak

To speak is to live

And to live is to revolt

And to live is to revolt

And to revolt is to dream....

10. A STAB TO THE BACK

When he lay to see her face

He thought about a time

When poison was more fruitful to him than wine

He didn't hold cups of wine

But poison was his only friend

Who invited him to a world called death

Death waited for him

Death wanted him

Death needed him

Death searched him

All he ever found was him

Holding the cup and drinking it

Death put his arms around his neck

Death answered all of his questions

Death gave him a peek into nothingness

And that's when shook his head

And put death down from his shoulders

He wished to see the skies

He wished to taste the wine

He wished to see her

Puppy or not

He stood for her

Human or alien

He fought for them

He wanted everything yet nothing

Death still lurks him from time to time

It's always the human who decides

Death or breath

11. Her pink scarf and white teeth's

Sounds at its peak

A high he never felt before

Her arms was just behind him

But he couldn't stop his legs to move around
and see her

He planned stories, poems and prayers to say to
her but couldn't

Her fingers touched his woollen shirt

Meanwhile he yearned to feel her lips and to
explore her back with a big old hug

Like an old man facing death he was satisfied for
that moment and that moment only

Her words still remain

Meanwhile he couldn't say a single word

Lost in his own words and worlds

A place hope is filled in cups

A place where hope is the intoxication

Smokes and drinks ahead

He wished for this day to be here once again

www.ingramcontent.com/pod-product-compliance
Lightning Source LLC
Chambersburg PA
CBHW031256130726
47988CB00008B/3376